One and Three by Nature

How the Trinity Defines Christianity

Brian Stanley Douglas

Copyright 2015, Brian Stanley Douglas.
All rights reserved.

ISBN: 978-0-578-43604-3

Special thanks to Elke Weesjes-Sabella, my friend and former colleague at Sussex University, for her input and encouragement on this project.

To read more by the author, visit www.brianstanleydouglas.com

To my son, Iain

You are wonderful

When all of its various sects and denominations are added together, Christianity is the largest faith group in the world. According to Pew Foundation research, about one in three persons alive today professes to be a Christian,[1] and the number of Christians in the world grows steadily each year. Yet despite its monolithic size, Christianity is an incredibly diverse faith that has manifested itself in disparate ways across time and geography. A first-time observer of Christian worship would think the medieval-style vespers of the ancient

---

[1] The Pew Foundation, "The Global Religious Landscape: A Report on the Size and Distribution of the World's Major Religious Groups as of 2010", http://www.pewforum.org/global-religious-landscape-exec.aspx, last accessed 21 July 2015.

cathedrals of Europe, for example, has very little in common with the energetic preaching of an African Methodist Episcopal church in the American Deep South, the culturally syncretized worship of a Sudanese village church, or the 100,000-member megachurches of Korea.[2]

Can each of these and the thousands of other expressions of Christianity be considered one faith? If so, what unifies Christianity

---

[2] Five of the ten largest Protestant churches in the world at present are found in South Korea. For examples of the diversity of Christianity in contemporary practice, see *The Economist*, "O Come All Ye Faithful", 1 Nov 2007. For more on the diversity of Christian history, see Adrian Hastings, ed., *A World History of Christianity* (Grand Rapids, MI: Eerdmans, 1999).

despite its diverse manifestations? While numerous beliefs and events have served to unify Christians at various times over the centuries, this essay will argue that one doctrine in particular—the doctrine of the Trinity—has been the most important and defining doctrine of the Christian faith throughout its history. It has served as a rallying point, at times uniting groups that were otherwise sharply opposed, and it has provided a foundation for Christianity's philosophical, political, and cultural contributions to world culture.

In short, this essay contends that *Christianity is Trinitarianism*—that is, the doctrine of the Trinity has historically and philosophically defined Christianity itself, even given Christianity its distinct 'Christianness'. While Christianity has at various times been deeply concerned (or unconcerned) with ethical, political, racial, cultural, economic, and environmental concerns, it is at its root a *theology*, which literally means a belief about God. Nothing is more definitive of Christianity as a religion than its beliefs about God, and the essence of the historic Christian belief about God is the doctrine of the Trinity. According to twentieth-century Swiss theologian Karl Barth,

> The doctrine of the Trinity is what basically distinguishes the Christian doctrine of God as Christian, and therefore what already distinguishes the Christian concept of revelation as Christian, in

contrast to all other possible doctrines of God or concepts of revelation.[3]

Or as historical theologian Gregg Allison wrote, belief in the Trinity 'distinguishes Christianity from all other religions of the world, including Judaism, Islam, Hinduism, and Buddhism. No other religion comes close to having a belief in a triune God, and some explicitly deny this cardinal truth of Christianity.'[4] If Barth and Allison are correct, then Christianity is, at its essence,

---

[3] Karl Barth, *Church Dogmatics* (Peabody, MA: Hendrickson, 2010), I/1.301.

[4] Gregg Allison, *Historical Theology* (Grand Rapids, MI: Zondervan, 2011), 231.

Trinitarianism. But is it true, and has it always been that way? And how should this equation shape our contemporary understanding of Christianity?

The classic articulation of the doctrine of the Trinity is that *the God of the Bible is one God but three persons*—that is, the Father, Son, and Holy Spirit are each distinct persons but they are one divine nature. This articulation affirms the singularity of monotheism but adds to it a diversity and complexity that is unique among the world religions. Limitations of size and scope prevent us from here evaluating whether that articulation of the doctrine of the Trinity is, in fact, taught in the Bible[5] or whether it

---

[5] Since the word 'Trinity' is not, after all,

is logically consistent. Those evaluations have been made by many and disputed by others over the centuries. The focus here will instead be on the primacy of the Trinity in Christian history, thought, and practice.

---

found in the Bible.

I. How the Trinity has Shaped Christian History

Although there have been dissenters in every age, there have been two major periods in the history of the church, each spanning about four hundred years, when the doctrine of the Trinity has seen its most focused and formidable challenges. In each instance the classic articulation of the Trinity has won out and been confirmed as the definitive Christian understanding of God. All rival theologies have been relegated to heterodoxy.

The story of the development of the doctrine of the Trinity begins in the era of the Fathers of the church, approximately AD 100-450. In this earliest age of Christianity, theologians debated over the nature of God as they tried to understand the person of Jesus. The confession of Jesus as Lord caused a division in the church: 'Jewish Christians, with their strong doctrine of the oneness of God, which they were not, of course, expected to renounce, inevitably tended to think of Christ as subordinate to the Father,' while Gentile converts, on the other hand, 'might have been tempted to solve the problem polytheistically, but the monotheistic core of the Christian message closed this path.'[6] According to historian Diarmaid MacCullogh,

---

[6] Geoffrey K. Bromiley, *Historical Theology* (Grand Rapids: Eerdmans, 1978), 68.

The Church spent its first four centuries arguing about how this could be. It needed to reconcile its story of a triune God made human with both its Jewish heritage of monotheism and with its Greek heritage from Plato, who said that the ultimate reality of a perfect God could have nothing to do with the confused, messy imperfection of the human world.[7]

The earliest extant articulations of the Trinity, which emerged within a century of the death of the last apostle,[8] focused

---

[7] Diarmaid MacCullogh, *The Reformation: A History* (New York: Penguin, 2003), 185.

[8] According to church tradition, St John

more on the practical workings of the three divine persons—especially their roles in the salvation of believers—than on a description of the nature of God. These early Trinitarians[9] described the Father's decree of salvation, the Son's sacrifice to secure it, and the Spirit's application of salvation to the individual believer. However, they did not directly account the relationship between the three

---

was the last apostle to die (c. 100 AD) and the only apostle to die of natural causes -- the others were all martyred for their faith.

[9] E.g., Athenagoras of Athens (c. 130-190): *A Plea for the Christians* (c. 177); Irenaeus of Lyon (c. 130-202): *Contra Haereses* (c. 180). According to church tradition, Irenaeus was a student of Polycarp of Smyrna, who was himself a student of the Apostle John.

persons and thus only indirectly addressed the doctrine of the Trinity as it was later more fully articulated.

It was Tertullian of Carthage (c. 160-c. 225), the first major Latin-speaking and -writing theologian,[10] who coined the term Trinity and first summarized it as a doctrine of God:

> '[Tertullian] provided the church with several essential terms and concepts. Beginning simply, he first described the Son and the Spirit exclusively in terms of their roles in the plan or "economy" of God. This... emphasizes the unity of God: there is only one divine

---

[10] *Adversus Praxean* (c. 213).

substance, one divine power, without separation division, dispersion, or diversity. At the same time, Tertullian emphasized distribution of functions, a distinction of Persons, a disposition or dispensation of the tasks. The deity is one substance, but not a numerical entity [of one].'[11]

The 'Cappadocian Fathers'[12] further contributed an emphasis on the inherent mystery of the Trinity: 'Cappadocian theology reflects an

---

[11] Harold O.J. Brown, *Heresies: Heresy and Orthodoxy in the History of the Church* (Peabody, MA: Hendrickson, 1998), 149.

[12] Basil of Caesarea (c. 330-379), Gregory of Nazianzus (c. 329-389), and Gregory of Nyssa (c. 335-c. 395).

ambiguity that is present in the New Testament itself. At times the expression "God" is used in a way that implies all three Persons of the Trinity, but at other times it is used to mean the Father alone.'[13] Gregory of Nyssa, for example, taught that '"we cannot, of course, express the ineffable depth of the mystery [of the Trinity] in words." Nevertheless, we can have some apprehension of the distinction of persons and unity of nature...'[14]

Even as the Church Fathers developed their expressions of the doctrine of the Trinity during the first through fifth centuries,[15] other early

---

[13] Brown, 153.

[14] Bromiley, 139.

[15] Clement of Rome (? - 99): *Epistle of*

theologians questioned the Trinity. Numerous counter-proposals were made as theologians struggled to understand and articulate the nature of God, and especially the person of Jesus: who was Jesus, was he God or man, and what was his relationship to the Father?[16] The most prominent

---

Clement (c. 97); Mathetes (dates unknown): *Epistle to Diognetus* (130); Justin Martyr (c. 100-165): *Dialogue with Trypho* (c. 160); Athanasius (c. 297-373): *De Incarnatione Verbi Dei* (c. 317) and *De Decretis* (367); Augustine (354-430): *De Trinitate* (c. 417).

[16] E.g., the Ebionites and Adoptionists (both second and third centuries) considered Jesus to be only human and not divine. Sabellius (dates unknown—third century) taught that the Father, Son, and Spirit were only varying manifestations of the one person of God. Apollinarius of Laodicea (?-390) and the Docetists (second and third centuries) held that Jesus was divine but not really

and influential Nontrinitarian in the early church was Arius of Alexandria (256-336), who taught that the Son was created by and consequently less than the Father, but superior to all else in creation and therefore ruler over all.

In response to all the conflicting beliefs in early Christianity, especially Arianism, the church held a series of councils to determine the biblical teaching on the nature of God. The Councils of

---

> human. The Monophysitists (fourth and fifth centuries) believed that Jesus was something of a divine-human hybrid, not fully either one but a third kind of being. Nestorius of Constantinople (c. 386-450) taught that Christ was actually two people, the man Jesus and the divine Son of God, who were distinct persons but existed together.

Nicaea (325), Constantinople (381), Ephesus (431), and Chalcedon (451) each produced a series of creeds, which were developed, according to historian E. Calvin Beisner, more out of religious experience than philosophical necessity:

> Unlike pure philosophical discussion, the creeds invariably had to do with the heart of the experience of Christians. They were not formulated for the sake of intellectual stimulation or exercise, but to explain why Christians experienced one thing and not another in their social and spiritual lives.[17]

---

[17] E. Calvin Beisner, *God in Three Persons*

All of the early councils and the creeds they produced—Apostle's, Nicene, Athanasian, Chalcedonian, and others—were distinctly and emphatically Trinitarian. All Nontrinitarian theology was designated heterodoxy, outside the bounds of Christianity, and the Trinity became the central doctrine that unified early Christianity, the definitive line in the sand that demarcated Christian and non-Christian beliefs. While there was a wide variety of practice concerning other doctrines, the doctrine of the Trinity became a fixed point of reference: Trinitarianism was the Christianity of the early church.[18]

(Wheaton, IL: Tyndale, 1984), 15.

[18] For more on the development of the

In the millennium following the Church Fathers, the doctrine of the Trinity was only infrequently challenged. The Trinity remained the definitive concept of God, most of the major theologians of the era contributed to its development as a doctrine,[19] and the few

---

doctrine of the Trinity in the ancient church, see Jaroslav Pelikan, *The Christian Tradition* (Chicago: University of Chicago, 1971), vol. 1, ch. 4 & 5; J.N.D. Kelly, *Early Christian Doctrines* (Peabody, MA: Hendrickson, 2003), ch. 5 & 9-12; Robert Letham, *The Holy Trinity: In Scripture, History, Theology, and Worship* (Phillipsburg, NJ: P&R, 2004), ch. 4-9.

[19] E.g., Boethius (c. 480-525): *De Trinitate* (c. 520); Anselm of Canterbury (c. 1033-1109): *Epistolae de Incarnatione Verbi* (1094); Richard of St. Victor (?-1173): *De Trinitate* (c. 1170); Thomas Aquinas (1225-74): *Summa Theologica* (1265-74), I.27-43; John Duns Scotus (c. 1266-

Nontrinitarian dissenters[20] played only a secondary role in church history. Somewhere between the dissenters and the defenders were the unfortunate Peter Abelard (1079-1142)[21] and Gilbert de la Porrée (c. 1075-1154),[22] who wrote to defend the historic doctrine of the Trinity but were judged by their contemporaries to have run afoul of it and consequently condemned. An

---

1308): see Pathernius Minges, ed., *Scoti Doctrina Philosophica et Theologica* (Rome: Collegii S. Bonaventurae, 1930), vol II.

[20] E.g., Roscellin of Compiègne (c. 1050-c. 1125); Joachim of Flora (c. 1135-1202).

[21] *Tractatus de Unitate et Trinitate Divina* (1121).

[22] *Commentarius in Boetium de Trinitate* (1225).

ongoing dispute over the 'Filioque clause' in the Nicene Creed contributed to the Great Schism between the East and West churches in 1054, but this was a dispute over how to best articulate the doctrine of the Trinity, which itself was never in question.[23]

The second period of challenge to the doctrine of the Trinity began during the Reformation. The 'Magisterial' Reformers (Luther, Calvin, et al) taught and the Anabaptists especially emphasized the 'priesthood of all

---

[23] For more on the development of the doctrine of the Trinity in the Medieval era, see Richard Muller, *Post-Reformation Reformed Dogmatics* (Grand Rapids: Baker, 2003), vol. 4, ch. 1; Letham, ch. 10-11.

believers'—that each believer has a personal relationship with God unmediated by the Church—which led to a democratization of religious thinking in which individuals shape their own theological beliefs rather than accepting the authoritative dogma of the Church. A consequence of this democratization was the emergence of a series of Nontrinitarian challengers,[24] who associated the various ancient councils and creeds that had

---

[24] E.g., Martin Cellarius (1499-1564): *De Operabus Dei* (1527); Michael Servetus (1509-53): *De Trinitatis Erroribus* (1531), *Dialogorum de Trinitate* (1532), and *Christianismi Restitutio* (1553); Fausto Sozzini (1539-1604) and his followers, the Socinians of Poland: *De Auctoritate Scripturae Sacrae* (1570), *De Jesu Christo Servatore* (1578), and *Racovian Catechism* (1605).

formulated the doctrine of the Trinity with the Roman Catholic Church. Their distrust for Rome and their desire to construct a new humanistic foundation for knowledge (in opposition to the church's dogmatic authority as the source of knowledge) caused them to question the Trinity.

As the Protestant and Catholic divisions led to often-violent conflicts across Europe in the sixteenth and seventeenth centuries, the two sides were united only by their belief in the Trinity. Protestants and Catholics alike persecuted Nontrinitarians across Europe, including Michael Servetus's persecution by Catholics in Vienna and subsequent execution by Protestants in Geneva in 1553. Despite their various theological and practical disagreements, all the major Reformers and all the major councils and creeds of the sixteenth and seventeenth centuries reaffirmed the Trinity, including Trent (1545-63), Dordt (1618-19), and Westminster (1643-49). Thus the Trinity was the one unifying doctrine between Catholics and Protestants—all Nontrinitarian thought was reaffirmed as heterodoxy, and Trinitarianism was the Christianity of the Reformation.

Those reaffirmations of the Trinity, however, did not settle the matter, and the doctrine was challenged again in the following centuries. For example, Baruch Spinoza (1632-77),[25] Baron

---

[25] *Korte Verhandeling van God, de mensch en deszelvs welstand* (c. 1660),

d'Holbach (1723-89),[26] Joseph Priestley (1733-1804),[27] and other figures of the 'Radical Enlightenment,' to borrow Jonathan Israel's term,[28] branched off from some of the more moderate Enlightenment writers[29] to directly

---

Ethica Ordine Geometrico Demonstrata (1677).

[26] *Lettres à Eugénie* (1768), *De la Cruauté Réligieuse* (1769), *Le Bon Sens* (1772), and others.

[27] *An History of the Corruptions of Christianity* (1782) and *Theological Repository* (1770–73, 1784–88).

[28] Cf. Jonathan Israel, *Radical Enlightenment* (Oxford: OUP, 2001), *Enlightenment Contested* (Oxford: OUP, 2009), *Democratic Enlightenment* (Oxford: OUP, 2011).

[29] E.g., Descartes, Locke, Hume, and Kant, who were themselves not necessarily Trinitarians, nonetheless typically

challenge the philosophical and theological status quo. The fiercely independent Radicals vigorously critiqued the historical teachings of Christianity, saving their sharpest assessments for those doctrines that they believed were irrational, like the Trinity and miracles. The spread of their influence and the rise of Unitarianism across Europe and America in the eighteenth and nineteenth centuries demonstrates a widespread, if not mainstream, acceptance of Nontrinitarian thought in the Post-Reformation.

As a response to the new theologies that arose from the

---

worked within the academic and social institutions of their day, in contrast to the Radicals.

Radical Enlightenment, the idea of 'cult' churches and theologies developed in mainstream Christian circles in the nineteenth century. The distinction between mainstream Christian sects or denominations (groups that differ on doctrines of secondary importance but affirm the historic Christian faith as defined by the major ecumenical creeds[30]) and 'cults' (groups that claim to be Christian, but do not affirm the ecumenical creeds), even to the present day, has typically centered on the doctrine of the Trinity. As Allison states it, 'a distinguishing characteristic of most sects and cults claiming to be Christian is a heretical belief about this matter [the

---

[30] The Apostle's, Nicene, Chalcedonian, and Athanasian Creeds.

Trinity].'[31] Though the beliefs and practices of mainstream denominations have varied widely, they are still considered 'Christian' by most; but to cross the Trinitarian line invariably results in being designated outside historic Christianity and a cult. It is for their Nontrinitarian theology that some have labeled as cults such groups as Christadelphians, Christian Scientists, Unitarian Universalists, Mormons, Jehovah's Witnesses, Iglesia ni Cristo, and "Oneness" Pentecostals.

According to some historical theologians, other theological controversies have caused the Trinity to be neglected or relegated to

---

[31] Allison, 231.

secondary importance in Post-Reformation theological discourse. The development of the historical-critical method of biblical interpretation in the nineteenth and twentieth centuries,[32] for example, generated a textual debate that undermined traditional biblical foundations of the doctrine of the Trinity and turned many theologians' attention elsewhere. By the twentieth century, the Trinity was so infrequently discussed that theologian Karl Rahner remarked, 'We must be willing to admit that,

---

[32] Initiated by Desiderius Erasmus (1466-1536) and Baruch Spinoza (1632-77), then more fully developed by F.C. Baur (1792-1860) and the Tübingen School of Theology, Adolf von Harnack (1851-1930), Ruldolph Bultmann (1884-1976), and others.

should the doctrine of the Trinity have to be dropped as false, the major part of religious literature could well remain virtually unchanged.'[33] Over the last half-century, however, that trend has shifted somewhat due to the influence of several influential theologians who have deliberately centered their theologies on the Trinity.[34] That said, the second

---

[33] Quoted in Allison, 247.

[34] E.g., Karl Barth (1886-1968): *Church Dogmatics* I/1.295ff; Karl Rahner (1904-84), *The Trinity* (London: Continuum, 2001); Colin E. Gunton (1941-2003): *The One, The Three, and the Many* (Cambridge: Cambridge, 1993); Thomas F. Torrance (1913-2007): *The Trinitarian Faith* (Edinburgh: T&T Clark, 1988), *Trinitarian Perspectives* (Edinburgh: T&T Clark, 1994), and *The Christian Doctrine of God* (Edinburgh: T&T Clark, 1996); Jürgen Moltmann (1926-): *The Trinity and the Kingdom*

period of challenge to the Trinity, which began with the Reformation, extends to the present and is an ongoing discussion in contemporary Christian theology. Yet despite challenge or neglect, the Trinity remains the main identifying mark of historic, orthodox Christianity.

(Minneapolis: Augsburg Fortress, 1993); Wolfhard Pannenberg (1928-2014): *Systematic Theology* (Grand Rapids: Eerdmans, 1991), vol. 1, ch. 5. For more on the development of the doctrine of the Trinity in the past century, cf. Letham, ch. 13-16.

II. How the Trinity has Shaped Christian Thought

The doctrine of the Trinity is central to Christian thought, and it theologically and philosophically sets Christianity apart as a unique belief system. In his book *3 Theories of Everything*, Basel-based pastor and philosopher Ellis Potter posits that all religions articulate a similar trajectory in how they explain the fundamental spiritual reality of the universe: a perfect beginning, an imperfect present, and a means to restore perfection in the future, or 'home—away—home again.'[35] Potter

---

[35] Ellis Potter, *3 Theories of Everything* (Huemoz: Destinée Media, 2012), 4.

further suggests that all the religions of the world can be divided into three categories based on what they believe is the path 'home again,' and it is in these three categories that Christianity's philosophical uniqueness can be seen.

Potter names the first group of religions *Monism*, which emphasizes the fundamental unity of all things. According to Monism, all is one: unities are "stable and dependable," but diversities are "unstable and undependable."

> Monism argues that the original perfection is a perfect, changeless, eternal unity. We suffer because we have forgotten this original unity and live in an illusion of

diversity. The illusion may seem very real to us, but it's an illusion nevertheless. According to Monism, the solution to suffering is to remember and realize the perfect unity again.[36]

Potter categorizes Buddhism, Hinduism, Islam, and various New Age and other mystical beliefs as Monism.

Potter calls the second group of religions *Dualism* and includes Zoroastrianism, Taoism, Confucianism, *yin-yang*, Hegelian and Marxist dialectic, and even "the Force" in *Star Wars* in this category. Dualism understands the

---

[36] Potter, 9.

fundamental reality of all things in terms of opposites:

> If we look around at the world, we observe many opposites in our experience of life: light-dark, hot-cold, hard-soft, pleasure-pain, sharp-dull, up-down, sweet-bitter, wet-dry, male-female. The idea behind Dualism is that life is good when opposites are in proper balance, or are in harmony with each other, but we suffer when there is an imbalance or disharmony.[37]

While Potter repeatedly commends Monism and Dualism for

---

[37] Potter, 29.

their intrinsic beauty and extensive contributions to world culture and art, he critiques them as each being able to explain only half of reality: Monism can explain the fundamental unity of all things but not diversity, while Dualism can explain the diversities of the universe but not unity.

Potter contrasts the third religion, the *Trinitarianism* of Christianity, as affirming both unity and diversity. Because Christianity understands the original reality of the universe (God) to be both unity and diversity (Trinity), neither can be the source of evil or suffering. Thus from Potter's perspective, Christianity is uniquely able to affirm both the unity and the diversity of human experience:

If the original perfection is both unified and diversified, it means that when we experience unity in reality it shouldn't be a problem, and when we experience diversity in reality it shouldn't be a problem. In other words, unlike Monism, [Trinitarianism] does not regard diversity as the cause of suffering, and does not see the solution to suffering as involving a detachment from diversity. Also, unlike Dualism, [Trinitarianism] does not attempt to resolve suffering by balancing opposites. Instead, [Trinitarianism] sees variation and contrast as a part of the original perfection, as a normal part of reality itself.[38]

Historical theologian Harold Brown agrees with Potter on how the doctrine of the Trinity uniquely shapes the Christian understanding of God and therefore ultimate reality: 'If one has a concept of the eternal Trinity, one can readily understand that there is at least a measure of multiplicity and variety within ultimate and absolute Reality itself, i.e., within God.'[39] Beyond just the idea of God, Trinitarianism shapes all the other major loci of historic Christian theology as well. It is the foundation, for example, for the

---

[38] Potter, 39.

[39] Brown, 146-47.

Christian concept of the relationship between God and the created universe. Brown describes how the doctrine of the Trinity accounts for the Christian belief that God is relational or personal and yet independent:

> [The Trinity] is fundamental to the Christian conception of God as personal as well as transcendent.... Christianity teaches that God is complete in himself. He had no inner need to create in order, as it were, to fulfill himself. Consequently, his decision to create was an act of his free and sovereign will, not a necessary function of his

being.[40]

Trinitarianism also shapes Christian anthropology—the doctrine of the nature and purpose of humanity—and illuminates the relationship between humanity and God. As Brown describes that relationship,

> [The Trinity] also has vital implications for the Christian understanding of the nature and destiny of man.... [and] for our own idea of human nature and the ultimate destiny of human beings.... If we conceive of the Trinity as an ongoing, eternal fellowship and

---

[40] Brown, 146.

communication between distinct Persons, then we can at least begin to understand how the concept of an eternal, personal life for countless created beings such as ourselves does not trouble or disrupt the absolute tranquility of God in eternity. The reason is simple: because God is Three, he is, so to speak, used to communication and conversation, and does not demand absolute silence.[41]

These are only a few examples of how the Trinity permeates and shapes Christian thought. In its core ideas, both philosophically and

---

[41] Brown, 146-7.

theologically, Christianity is Trinitarianism, and that is what makes Christianity unique among world religions.[42]

---

[42] For an exceptional study on how the Trinity shapes Christian thought, see Colin Gunton's *The One, the Three, and the Many* (Cambridge: Cambridge UP, 1993).

III. How the Trinity has Shaped Christian Practice

From the earliest days of Christianity, the Trinity has not been just an abstract, academic, "behind-the-scenes" doctrine. Rather, it has shaped Christian practice both at the broader ecclesiastical level and for individual Christians. As Michael Reeves states it, 'Far from theological clutter, God's being Father, Son, and Spirit is just what makes the Christian life beautiful.'[43] That idea of a beautiful Trinitarian life has shaped Christian ideas of holiness and virtue, prayer, baptism, aesthetics,

---

[43] Reeves, 102.

apologetics, and the like.[44] This essay will focus on how the Trinity has shaped the Christian virtue of love.

The entire breadth of Christian practice—worship, justice, ethics, etc—has traditionally been rooted in what Jesus called the two Greatest Commandments: love the Lord your God, and love your neighbor.[45] This Christian idea of

---

[44] For more on how the doctrine of the Trinity has shaped Christian practice, see Allison, 232ff.; Letham, ch. 17-20; Fred Sanders, *The Deep Things of God: How the Trinity Changes Everything* (Wheaton, IL: Crossway, 2010); Michael Reeves, *Delighting in the Trinity* (Downers Grove, IL: IVP Academic, 2012); Sam Alberry, *Connected: Living in the Light of the Trinity* (Phillipsburg, NJ: P&R, 2012).

[45] Gospel of Matthew 22.35-40; Gospel of

love, however—whether for God or for neighbor—is founded on the nature of God since 'God is love'[46] and consequently the source from which the idea of love and practice of loving are derived. Yet the very concept of love assumes a plurality of persons: a solitary being is incapable of love because it is alone. It has nothing external to itself to love and nothing to offer love in return. If God is one person and not three, love would not be an essential, eternal attribute of the divine nature. The very idea of love would have no theological origin, and any command to love would be an arbitrary, pragmatic (temporary?)

Mark 12.28-31.

[46] Epistle of 1 John 4.8,16.

rule imposed on humanity.

Potter addresses this with his axiom, 'God alone is God, and God is not alone.'[47] The fact that the Christian God is Trinity provides a basis for love and its underlying concepts of personality and relationship. Because God has existed in personality, relationship, and love in eternity, Trinitarians believe, human persons, relationships, and love are to reflect the image of the Triune God.[48] Further, the way in which the three persons of the Trinity are believed to

---

[47] Potter, 38. Cf. Potter, 53-54.

[48] This idea of relationship and love as a reflection of God's image also underlies some Christian beliefs about gender. Cf. Genesis 1.26-27.

love each other provides an example of true love: the three persons are understood to be not in competition but united in their desires and goals—each is selfless and exists to serve the others. That is, the Father desires to glorify the Son and Spirit and acts accordingly; the Son is sent by and obeys the Father and seeks to glorify him; the Spirit is sent by the Father and the Son and will glorify them both.[49] The example of the Trinity is that love can only exist in relationship, and that true love is self-sacrificial rather than self-serving. This idea of selfless, relational love has in turn served as the traditional basis for Christian concepts of community, hospitality,

---

[49] Cf. Gospel of John, ch. 14, 16, 17.

service, justice, ethics, etc.

There has certainly been a diversity amongst Christians in their expressions of love (or lack thereof), as there has been a diversity in all categories of Christian practice. Sometimes these divergent practices have led to conflict and division, to the degree that there are approximately 41,000 distinct Christian organizations and denominations in the world today.[50] Christians over the centuries have disagreed about many things—

---

[50] The Pew Foundation, "Global Christianity: A Report on the Size and Distribution of the World's Christian Population" (2011), http://www.pewforum.org/Christian/Global-Christianity-movements-and-denominations.aspx, last accessed 21 July 2015.

perhaps even nearly everything at times. Yet throughout these disagreements, the Trinity's shaping influence is evident among the diverse manifestations of Christianity. Whether serving as the definitional boundary between historic orthodoxy and heterodoxy, or providing a foundation for the diversity of Christian thinking and practice, the Trinity has defined and unified Christianity across time and geography, which is why it is fair to say that Christianity equals Trinitarianism.

About the Author

Brian Stanley Douglas is husband to Jordan, father to one son & two daughters, and Associate Pastor at All Saints Presbyterian Church in Boise, Idaho. He grew up near Miami and spent a couple years in Brighton, UK before moving to Boise in 2008. Before becoming a pastor, he taught history, humanities, and political science at the high school and university levels. He has studied at Stetson University, Knox Seminary, Sussex University, and Boise State University and is a lifelong fan of the Detroit Tigers.

www.ingramcontent.com/pod-product-compliance
Lightning Source LLC
Chambersburg PA
CBHW022000290426
44108CB00012B/1148